Captured Miracles

Presents

THE *Miracle* OF
AMERICA
BIRTH OF A NATION

WRITTEN BY
BRIAN P. TROTTER
WILLIAM S. NORTON

FINE ART PHOTOGRAPHY BY
HELEN THOMAS ROBSON

Published by:

Captured Miracles Productions, www.CapturedMiracles.org

National Center for Constitutional Studies, www.NCCS.net

ISBN: 978-0-88080-166-9

www.CapturedMiracles.org

Printed in the United States of America

TABLE OF CONTENTS

FOREWORD

"We mutually pledge to each other our Lives, our Fortunes, and our Sacred Honor."

The men who signed the Declaration of Independence had no illusions about the consequences of signing that document. They knew full well what they risked and how much they pledged when they, with a firm reliance on God, put their names to the document and with faith proclaimed *"We are, and of right ought to be Free."*

On July 2, 1776, Washington, who had recently been appointed commanding General, sent a stirring communication to his men that the time for commitment had arrived, that Americans could no longer suffer complacently under Britain's tyrannical rule. Unbeknown to the General, on that very day Congress had voted unanimously in favor of a resolution for independence. (Two days later, on July 4, Congress approved the actual Declaration of Independence, which had been drafted by Thomas Jefferson.) Acting on his own instincts, Washington issued orders that said:

"The time is now near at hand which must determine whether Americans are to be freemen or slaves, whether they are to have any property they can call their own.... The fate of unborn millions will now depend, under God, on the courage and conduct of this army. Our cruel and unrelenting enemy leaves us no choice but a brave resistance.... We have therefore to resolve to conquer or die. Our own country's honor [calls] upon us.... Let us therefore rely upon the goodness of the cause, and the aid of the Supreme Being ... to ... encourage us to great and noble actions. The eyes of all our countrymen are now upon us, and we shall have their blessings and praises if, happily, we are the instrument of saving them from the tyranny meditated against them. Let us therefore ... show the whole world that a freeman contending for LIBERTY on his own ground is superior to any slavish mercenary on earth."

A fiery young patriot named Thomas Paine, by campfire light with a drumhead for a desk, penned a passage that later became enshrined in America's classics. He wrote:

"These are the times that try men's souls. The summer soldier and the sunshine patriot will, in this crisis, shrink from the service of their country;

but he that stands it now deserves the love and thanks of man and woman. Tyranny, like hell, is not easily conquered; yet we have this consolation with us, that the harder the conflict, the more glorious the triumph.... Heaven knows how to put a proper price upon its goods; and it would be strange indeed if so celestial an article as FREEDOM should not be highly rated."

It is interesting to observe that the number of real patriots is always very small compared to the whole population. A true patriot usually puts forth much more effort, anguish, and sacrifice than what most people, who later enjoy the benefits, will ever know. In 1776, there were more than three million residents in the 13 colonies. Washington's army had less than 10,000 men. That's less than one-half of one percent of the entire country. Where were the others? They were mostly enjoying the warmth of their homes with plenty to eat. Did they know what was happening to Washington? Probably not, but they benefited from Washington's actions.

A true patriot is always a pioneer. He is years ahead of most others in his vision and purpose. John Adams struggled to convince the Massachusetts legislature to adopt a three-branch government in his state, years before it became popular. Thomas Jefferson tried to free the slaves in Virginia years before they finally were.

A true patriot is willing to sacrifice his own life and fortune for the benefit of the cause. Of those 56 men who signed the Declaration of Independence, nine died of wounds or hardships during the war. Five were captured and imprisoned, in each case with brutal treatment. Several lost wives, sons or entire families. One lost his 13 children. Two wives were brutally treated. All were, at one time or another, the victims of manhunts and driven from their homes. Twelve signers had their homes completely burned. Seventeen lost everything they owned. Yet not one defected or went back on his pledged word.

This new book, *The Miracle of America, Birth of a Nation*, presented by Captured Miracles and the National Center for Constitutional Studies, has brought to life the miraculous events surrounding the founding of this great nation and its heritage. The fine art photography and stories bring the patriots of the past to their beneficiaries of today and inspire us to become the patriots of the future.

Earl Taylor, Jr.
President of National Center
for Constitutional Studies

PREFACE

The Miracle of America, Birth of a Nation began as Captured Miracles photographer, Helen Thomas Robson, attended a Making of America seminar presented by the National Center for Constitutional Studies (NCCS). She came away with a new appreciation for America and the many events and people that helped forge a nation that has blessed mankind as an example of freedom and prosperity. Feeling inspired by our forefathers, Helen decided to use her talents to recreate these events using fine art photography.* She soon enlisted her husband Rusty Robson and business partners Brian and Alison Trotter. They recruited Bill Norton, founder of Constitution Week USA and a presenter for NCCS, to help research the amazing stories and events found in this book. It was determined to create a collection of fine art photographs to highlight both known and lesser known stories to inspire hearts and minds to return to the founding principles of this great land.

After the first photo shoot for the Abigail Adams, Thomas Jefferson, and Reverend Thomas Prince pictures, it be-came clear that a photo shoot at Independence Hall would be a necessity. The Captured Miracles team and dozens of volunteers descended upon Knott's Berry Farm in Orange County, California. Wanting Americans in the West to have access to their heritage, Mr. Walter Knott built a brick-by-brick replica of Philadelphia's Independence Hall in 1966. True to Mr. Knott's character, the building curators graciously allowed the Captured Miracles team to use the building for a day-long photo shoot to capture the significant events that resulted in the Declaration of Independence and the U.S. Constitution.

"Though this is just a reenactment," one volunteer recalled, *"to be in a replica of the east room where the signing of those documents took place, and to be in the company of Franklin, Washington, Jefferson, Madison and others, it is most humbling."*

Of course they were just ordinary people dressing the part, but these volunteers had a spirit of commitment to the cause that brought a profound reverence to the day.

As the Miracle of America collection came together, organizers for Arizona's Celebration of Freedom requested that the collection be put on display during their event in July of 2010. In agreement, Captured Miracles decided that just showing these beautiful pictures wasn't enough. Brian and Bill worked night and day researching and writing the stories connected to the art. Kirsten Millsap, an extremely talented songwriter and vocalist, was recruited to write and arrange music to accompany the stories. With the combined talents of the Captured Miracles team, what started as an art collection developed into an amazing musical concert with some of the most talented vocalists and musicians in the country, spoken narration telling the beautiful history of America, and a visual art production that renews the spirit and carries the heritage of this land deep into the soul.

As teary-eyed patriots left the concert our mission was clear. This message must be shared with Americans young and old. As a result, it is our honor and privilege to present to you, in book form, a few of the events and people that made this nation great. We hope you enjoy it as much as we have. Visit our web site at www.CapturedMiracles.org to learn how you can help us spread the beautiful message of *"The Miracle of America, Birth of a Nation."*

*Fine Art Photography is an artistic medium that begins with one or more traditional photographs. These photos go through a process of digital manipulation by the artist to express a message or stir specific emotions. Fine art photography is often mistaken for paintings or other artistic mediums.

Captured Miracles

EXTENDS A SPECIAL THANKS TO:

Our Battle Cry

Let us put aside our differences and come together as believers in a Creator—That we are a moral people and a nation united under God, with the ability to achieve miracles.

THE *Miracle* OF
AMERICA
BIRTH OF A NATION

A merica has a rich heritage of God-fearing and freedom-loving pioneers who blazed a trail of Liberty that has been a blessing to the world. They bought freedom with their life's blood for generations unknown to them in their minds but hoped for in their hearts.

The settlement of America began with a few small bands of struggling victims of an oppressed existence seeking for the freedom to worship God according to their own dictates, not the dictates of tyrants. *"When, in the course of human events,"* as the Declaration of Independence declares, *"it becomes necessary for one people to dissolve the political bands which have connected them with another, and to assume, among the powers of the earth, the separate and equal station to which the laws of nature and of nature's God entitle them, . . . requires that they should declare the causes which impel them to the separation.*

"We hold these truths to be self-evident, that all men are created equal, that they are endowed by their Creator with certain unalienable rights, that among these are life, liberty, and the pursuit of happiness."

Miracle AT THE
OLD SOUTH CHURCH

———❖———

*I*n modern day Massachusetts, there resides the famous Old South Church, an historic edifice that once was the tallest building in all of Boston. Now, it sits quietly nestled in the midst of the towering office buildings of busy urban life. But this unassuming church holds a secret: an amazing story of faith and Divine intervention.

In October of 1746, during what came to be known as King George's War, France sent a fleet of nearly 100 ships to burn the coastal cities of America.

The American colonists alone held no hope in matching the massive cannon, gun and manpower of this great fleet. They needed a miracle! The governor of Massachusetts assembled what men and resources he could and called for a universal day of fasting and prayer. Thronging to the churches, people everywhere pleaded with the Almighty asking for that miracle.

Time was short as the fleet was quickly approaching their shores. The Reverend Thomas Prince, from the high pulpit of the Old South Church, prayed before hundreds. He offered up these very words:

"Deliver us from our enemy! Send Thy tempest, Lord, upon the waters to the eastward! Raise Thy right hand. Scatter the ships of our tormentors and drive them hence. Sink their proud frigates beneath the power of Thy winds!"

He had scarcely pronounced the words when the sun was consumed by darkness and there arose a great tempest in the sea. The land was cast in shadow, as a great wind arose. Suddenly, the shutters began a violent hammering—slamming at the windows as if the very hand of God shook the earth. The bell in the tower atop the old church began to ring erratically.

Reverend Prince raised his hands high above his head, *"We hear thee! We hear Thy voice, O Lord! We hear it! Thy breath is upon the waters to the eastward, even upon the deep. Thy bell tolls for the death of our enemies!"*

He bowed his head in reverence, then looked up, tears streaming down his face. *"Thine be the glory, Lord. Amen and amen!"*

The following week would bring news that a miracle had occurred—a virtual hurricane had risen out of the Atlantic and sunk nearly all of those French frigates. The remaining ships were observed sailing, broken and battered, from whence they came.

Boston wasn't burned! Charleston wasn't burned! New York wasn't burned! God had once again preserved the colonists from utter destruction.

"Miracle at The Old South Church"

*T*he trials and difficulty found in this and other accounts groomed the American colonists into a people strong, full of courage, possessing humility and faith. These faithful colonists were the generation that raised the Founding Fathers and prepared them for a divine mission. Their younger years shaped them for this very purpose.*"As the sapling goes, so grows the tree."*

THE *Bulletproof* GEORGE WASHINGTON

One such event brings us to the Battle of the Monongahela on July 9, 1755, where we find a young lieutenant colonel, George Washington, who was serving in the British army.

"Foolishness!" the Indian chief exclaimed, as he gazed scornfully across the battlefield. From their hiding places the French and Indian warriors could see the British soldiers dressed in their bright red uniforms, shoulder to shoulder; 1500 men marching down the forest road to their death, like a grove of small trees waiting to be chopped to the ground.

The British were trained for European battle and stood little chance against the French and Indian guerilla warfare.

Fully exposed atop their horses, British officers attempted to hold their men in formation even as the Indian warriors shot them one by one.

The slaughter ensued for two hours.

"Quick! Let your aim be certain, and he dies!" the chief commanded.

The warriors leveled their rifles at Washington — round after round, bullet after bullet; smoke filled the forest. Twice his horse was shot from beneath him. As horses were left by the death of fellow officers, he mounted them and continued to crisscross the battlefield carrying orders to the soldiers. More rounds fired, the sharpshooters taking one life after another. Nearly 1000 young men were killed, and still, Lieutenant Colonel Washington remained.

The native warriors stared in disbelief. Their rifles seldom missed their mark.

"Stop firing!" the Chief commanded. *"This one is under special protection of the Great Spirit."*

Another Indian warrior added, *"I had seventeen clear shots at this man . . . and after all, could not bring him to the ground. This man was not born to be killed by the bullet."*

As the firing slowed, Washington gathered the remaining troops and retreated to safety. That evening, he noticed an odd tear in his coat. It was a bullet hole! He rolled up his sleeve and looked at his arm directly under the hole. There was no mark upon his skin. Amazed, he took off his coat to find three more holes where bullets had passed through the fabric, never piercing his skin. The life of George Washington had been miraculously spared.

PRESERVED FOR A *Greater* PURPOSE
GEORGE WASHINGTON

Fifteen years later, in 1770, George Washington returned to the sacred grounds of the same Pennsylvania woods. The Indian chief heard that Washington was in the area and traveled many days to meet with him.

Over a blazing council fire, the chief told Washington the following:

"I am a chief and ruler over my tribes. My influence extends to the waters of the great lakes and to the far Blue Mountains. I have traveled a long and weary path that I might see the young warrior of the great battle. It was on the day when the white man's blood mixed with the streams of our forests that I first beheld this chief. . . . Our rifles were leveled, rifles which, but for you, knew not how to miss— 'twas all in vain; a power mightier far than we shielded you. . . . Seeing you were under the special guardianship of the Great Spirit, we immediately ceased to fire. I am old and shall soon be gathered to the land of the shades, but ere I go, there is something bids me speak in the voice of prophecy—Listen!

"The Great Spirit protects that man and guides his destinies—he will become the chief of nations, and a people yet unborn will hail him as the founder of a mighty empire. I am come to pay homage to the man who is the particular favorite of Heaven, and who can never die in battle."

Nine days after the battle, having heard a rumor of his own death, the young George Washington wrote his brother to inform him that he was still alive.

"Preserved For A Greater Purpose"

"As I have heard since my arrival at this place, a circumstantial account of my death and dying speech, I take this early opportunity of contradicting the first and of assuring you that I have not as yet composed the latter. But by the all-powerful dispensations of Providence I have been protected beyond all human probability or expectation; for I had four bullets through my coat, and two horses shot under me yet escaped unhurt, although death was leveling my companions on every side of me!"

In all the battles that followed in his long military career, George Washington was never wounded in battle.

Until 1934, the story of the "Bulletproof George Washington" could be found in every school textbook. Now it has been read by few Americans. Washington often reflected on this significant event that formed his character and confirmed his calling. Washington was indeed prepared in character and reputation to fulfill an important role in the birth of a nation.

WITH *Humility* I ACCEPT
GEORGE WASHINGTON

April 18, 1775 brought news that the British Army had fired upon the American militia, and thereby started the American Revolution.

During the second meeting of the Continental Congress, news of the bloodshed came with the realization that settling matters without conflict would be impossible.

One of the first steps of the new Congress was to adopt the army gathered about Boston, calling it the Continental Army.

It then became necessary to give that body a leader—a commander-in-chief to handle it. Opinions varied; several were ambitious for the post. George Washington was nominated by John Adams, who was recorded as saying:

"With Humility I Accept"

"I had no hesitation to declare, I had but one gentleman in my mind for that important command... and that was a gentleman from Virginia whose skill and experience as an officer and excellent universal character would unite the colonies better than any other person in the union."

The following day from his place in the assembly, George Washington accepted the appointment in a brief speech, in which he said:

"I beg you will accept my cordial thanks for this distinguished testimony of your approval... I beg it may be remembered by every gentleman in the room that I this day declare with the utmost sincerity I do not think myself equal to the command I am honored with. As to pay, Gentlemen, I do not wish to make any profit from it."

And so it was, with his instructions and a packet of commissions, General Washington made preparations to leave for Boston.

> *"... I do not think myself equal to the command I am honored with. As to pay, Gentlemen, I do not wish to make any profit from it."*
>
> —George Washington

"Dearest John"

BUILDING *A* FUTURE
JOHN & ABIGAIL ADAMS

The nomination of George Washington came from John Adams, a man polished by a family devoted to the cause of liberty—his own father had been present when Reverend Prince gave his stirring prayer in the Old South Church. John and his wife Abigail were committed to justice and all that was right, but their tasks weighed heavily upon their shoulders and often required long absences from one another. Many of their letters of support, love and encouragement were preserved and give us a glimpse into this pioneering and dedicated couple.

12

Dearest John,

It feels as though we have spent a far greater portion of our marriage apart than together. Strange how the sun rises and sets whether you be at my side or not. But in this cause we build a future, it is our legacy— freedom is the best gift we can impart to our children. We shall fight for the rights of men and women, and shall prevail against those who would deny us this agency. I possess no doubt, that with God on our side, we shall have no need to fear what mortal men can do.

All my love
Abigail

"My Dear Abigail"

$\mathcal{D}$earest John,

It feels as though we have spent a far greater portion of our marriage apart, than together. Strange how the sun rises and sets whether you be at my side or not. But in this cause we build a future—it is our legacy—freedom is the best gift we can impart to our children. We shall fight for the rights of men and women, and shall prevail against those who would deny us this agency. I possess no doubt, that with God on our side, we shall have no need to fear what mortal men can do.

All my love, *Abigail*

$\mathcal{M}$y Dear Abigail,

It is hard indeed to be apart. The price we pay is dear—I marvel that our family remains intact and strong despite this grievous distance, and we both know the dire consequence we will face if we are unsuccessful in our endeavors—but this good work is ours to do—for in our sacrifice we lay the foundation of a nation that will endow all men with equality and the ability to reach their greatest potential—and fill the measure of their creation!

All my love, *John*

On June 11, 1776, John Adams was one of five delegates appointed to begin drafting a declaration of independence. When the task came down to Thomas Jefferson or John Adams, Jefferson proposed that Adams make the draft.

To which John Adams answered, *"I will not. You should do it."*

"Oh, no!" Jefferson exclaimed, *"Why will you not? You ought to do it."*

"I will not!" Adams replied.

"Why?" said Jefferson.

Adams answered, *"Reasons enough."*

"What can be your reasons?" queried Jefferson.

Adams gave him three. *"Reason first—You are a Virginian, and a Virginian ought to appear at the head of this business. Reason second—I am obnoxious, suspected, and unpopular. You are very much otherwise. Reason third—You can write ten times better than I can."*

"Well," Jefferson said, *"if you are decided, I will do as well as I can."*

AN *Inspired* WORK
THOMAS JEFFERSON
THE DECLARATION OF INDEPENDENCE

1776 was a very difficult year for the Americans. It was a particularly difficult year for Thomas Jefferson. Within months of the death of his daughter, his beloved mother passed away, and his wife became extremely ill. His concern over the fate of his country and the state of Virginia gave him severe migraine headaches that would last for weeks at a time. But Thomas Jefferson was not a man easily deterred—no matter the adversity, he pressed forward in his determination to see America's liberation from British rule.

These were the conditions of Jefferson's life when he came to be the author of the Declaration of Independence. For 17 days he wrestled with the task of laying on paper the fundamental *"Ancient Principles,"* the laws of nature and of nature's God. Jefferson felt the weight of this profound responsibility, and in the face of much personal distress, he forged ahead.

In moments of self-doubt, Jefferson, an accomplished violinist, would often turn to the instrument to calm his mind and clear his thoughts.

As he would play, anxiety would fade and inspiration would again flood into his mind, enabling his pen to drip with inspiration upon the page.

Once completed, Jefferson communicated the document first to John Adams and Benjamin Franklin, requesting their wisdom because, he said, *"They were the two members of whose judgments and amendments I wished most to have the benefit. . . . Their alterations were two or three only."*

A LIGHT TO ALL *Mankind*
THE DECLARATION OF INDEPENDENCE

With no further alterations to the Declaration by the committee, the sacred document was presented to John Hancock and the rest of the Continental Congress, where it met with a storm of debate. Tossed to and fro, this fragile document finally rested on the reverent waters of calm, where among the many changes made, none were found to alter the *"ancient principles"* that Jefferson had worked so hard to document. These principles would now sit perched upon a hill as a light to all mankind.

The words laid on that parchment over two centuries ago were not mere rhetoric, but represented a genuine commitment to original principles—a commitment that was tested on the battlefields of Liberty, as the signers, with a firm reliance on the protection of Divine Providence, mutually pledged to each other their Lives, their Fortunes, and their sacred Honor. This became very real as the Revolutionary War overshadowed the land with the might of the British Empire.

It was not yet settled; the vote on the Declaration still needed to be taken. The Continental Congress pressed for Independence. They knew the realization of the American dream would require that the document be a unanimous Declaration of Independence, among all 13 colonies, but the two delegates from Delaware were deadlocked and the third, Caesar Rodney, was not in Philadelphia. With a true sense of urgency, a messenger was dispatched immediately to find Mr. Rodney.

"The *Sacrifice* Be Mine"
CAESAR RODNEY

The message no sooner reached him, than, laying aside all other engagements—including a much-needed voyage to England for a life-saving procedure for skin cancer—Caesar Rodney rode an exhausting eighty miles through the night during a torrential downpour, arriving in Philadelphia on July 2, 1776, just as the voting was beginning.

Rodney arrived lacerated and in much pain, but participated nonetheless *"in his boots and spurs."* This too was a man inflamed with the godly desire for freedom—he understood his role in the birth of a free nation, and would not be deterred from his course—no matter his personal cost.

Caesar Rodney's critical vote allowed Delaware to join the other colonies in making a unanimous vote for independence. His sacrifice would cost him his life however, for he would never fully recover from his nighttime ride through the storm, and in his weakened state, he succumbed to the skin cancer he had left untreated.

"The Sacrifice Be Mine"

$\mathcal{M}$r. Rodney's sacrifice is just one more example of the many sacrifices our forefathers made to ensure our generation would enjoy the freedoms they lacked. It is of particular note that if the war for independence had been lost, these good men and their families would have been tried for treason—the penalty for which was not just death, but far, far worse. After a horrifying and excruciatingly long process, when spirit and flesh had been unmercifully parted, their quartered remains would have been scattered across the countryside, so that their final resting place would be unknown, unnamed, and unhonored—and yet in spite of this threat, these stalwart men pursued their righteous path, pressing forward with faith in their Creator. We may ask ourselves—if the task rested upon our shoulders—*would you have signed it?*

BATTLE AT *King's* MOUNTAIN

Lord Cornwallis, elated with his victory at Camden, South Carolina, began his march toward North Carolina, his next step to complete victory.

Cornwallis' flank was protected by Major Patrick Ferguson—a soldier with a treacherous reputation—who pillaged and burnt the homes of American patriots. As Ferguson entrenched himself atop King's Mountain, an army of rugged men from the mountains of Tennessee surrounded him. In his arrogance, Ferguson proclaimed, *"Neither the rebels nor God Himself can dislodge me from atop this mountain."* Before the battle concluded, the Americans sent him back to his Maker to make peace with that statement—a statement that would prove to be prophetic, however, for neither God nor the rebels did dislodge him. He can still be found, atop that mountain, in a shallow grave right where he died.

The defeat at King's Mountain seriously blunted the British campaign in the south, and forced a frightened Cornwallis to abandon his plans and retreat to Yorktown.

AN UNCOMMON *Miracle*
EMILY GEIGER

———◄❖►———

*S*ome battles were fought by great soldiers and others by common people who fought and sacrificed for freedom in their own backyards.

John Geiger, a disabled American patriot was unable to serve his country; however, he instilled in his beautiful daughter Emily, a love of freedom and liberty. Emily, being a young woman, was frustrated by her inability to serve in the war effort. Her excitement could not be contained when the occasion presented itself to serve as a courier for General Nathanael Greene.

An opportunity for General Greene to launch an assault upon the British required an urgent dispatch be sent immediately to General Sumter, over one hundred miles away. Finding a willing man to carry the message would prove to be impossible. The route was considered a death sentence—the dense forest road was crawling with British and sympathetic Tories, yet Emily was eager to volunteer.

"One Hundred Miles"

Helen T Robson

Quietly, she took leave of her home and loved ones and made her way to General Greene's encampment, where she volunteered herself to carry the message. General Greene was extremely hesitant to expose the young girl to such danger. He explained that if caught, she could be tortured and hanged for treason. But this resolute young girl was willing to take the risk. With no other option, and with a heavy heart, General Greene wrote the dispatch, and sent her off to fulfill her dangerous mission.

The first evening, Emily, weary from travel, stopped at a farm house seeking directions. The mother of the home, seeing that Emily was in physical despair, insisted she rest for the night. Emily had been asleep for two hours when she was awakened by a voice at the door. She could hear the men through an open window asking for a young female spy with a hidden message. Emily quietly dressed herself and slipped out the second story window, dropped from the roof, and retrieved her horse from the barn, barely escaping into the night.

On the second day she was seized upon by three soldiers and transported to Lord Rawdon, who interrogated her. She, being young and innocent in the art of deception, left Lord Rawdon angry and suspicious. He locked her in the guardhouse and called for a matron to have her searched. Left alone for a brief moment, Emily quickly pulled the dispatch from her pocket, committed it to memory, tore it to pieces and began to eat it. She had scarcely finished the last bit when the matron appeared and searched her from head to toe, finding nothing of suspicion, Emily was finally released. She mounted her horse and despite her exhaustion, made haste riding through the night to reach General Sumter.

She arrived that morning, weak, thirsty and faint, but in reciting her message to the general, Emily Geiger completed her mission. It would be nearly two weeks before this brave girl would finally return to the safety of her father; within the quiet resolve of his sweet daughter, John Geiger would find an uncommon miracle—and so would America.

Emily's brave act of service proved pivotal to success over the British. With the combined strength of General Sumter and General Greene, the Americans launched an attack against Lord Rawdon and his forces, leaving them crippled and unable to join Cornwallis, who would face General Washington and the approaching French fleet on his own at Yorktown.

It is a strange phenomenon in history that often the triumph of a monumental victory comes close on the heels of what might have been a colossal defeat. It was so with Washington in 1781, when the midnight darkness of despair suddenly gave way to the incredible events which led to Yorktown.

CORNWALLIS' *Defeat* AT YORKTOWN

When Washington learned of the French plan to bring their fleet into Chesapeake Bay, rather than bring them to New York as originally planned, he seized the opportunity to trap Cornwallis.

He developed a masterful plan: while appearing to ready his men to recapture New York, he in fact prepared them for a forced march to Yorktown. This tactic was a remarkable success. Before the British knew what was happening, the French fleet had bottled up the entrance to the Chesapeake and sealed off Yorktown.

Cornwallis was trapped against the York River and there were no British ships to bring him supplies or evacuate his troops. With Lord Rawdon's and Major Ferguson's defeats, there were no other British forces to come to his aid. Thus the battle began.

After seven days and nights of fighting, the great Cornwallis made a desperate attempt to retreat across the York River. But it was not to be. Barely had his men loaded the boats to row across the river, when a mighty wind slammed the boats back to the river bank!

Cornwallis exclaimed that, *"It looked as if God Himself was on Washington's side!"*

On the morning of October 17, the guns fell silent, and the victory of the last major battle of the Revolutionary War went to the Americans.

Washington's reaction to the victory was typical of his nature. He earnestly recommended that all troops attend church services, and do so in a spirit of gratitude for the Divine Providence that had blessed them throughout the war.

"Cornwallis' Defeat at Yorktown"

"Washington's Worst Ordeal"

WASHINGTON'S *Worst* ORDEAL

Seven months after the battle at Yorktown, Washington received a most disturbing letter from one of his officers, outlining the military's grievances with Congress and the consideration of a possible military revolt. Congress had failed to honor its promises made to the army concerning salary and pensions. The officer pleaded with Washington to accept the crown and serve as King George I of the United States.

Horrified, Washington wrote back immediately, denouncing the idea. America had come too far to return to tyranny.

Washington's strong feelings did not pacify the rumbling restlessness of the military, which called for a military revolt with or without Washington. In a meeting of officers on the subject, Washington reviewed their grievances and expressed a determination to work with Congress for a just solution. Washington saw that the officers were still sullen and silent. Having failed to persuade them, he reached into his pocket and retrieved a letter from Congress explaining the financial difficulties of the government.

In their seats the officers shifted uncomfortably. Suddenly every heart missed a beat. Something was the matter with their commander. He seemed unable to read the paper. He paused in bewilderment. Fumbling in his waistcoat pocket, Washington took out a pair of reading glasses—something that only his closest friends had seen him wear. He then said quietly,

"Gentlemen, you will permit me to put on my spectacles,
for I have not only grown gray in the service of my country,
but blind also."

This simple statement achieved what all of Washington's arguments had been unable to accomplish. The officers were deeply moved and shed tears of affection. They had great admiration for their aging general, who had led them all so far and so long. Washington quietly finished reading the letter, walked out of the hall, mounted his horse, and disappeared from view.

Washington's officers realized that they had followed their leader into battle for the cause of Liberty and they would follow him again, into the next battle, to determine if they could become a self-governing people.

WASHINGTON *Resigns* HIS COMMISSION

The final treaty for peace between the United States and Britain was signed in the spring of 1783. America had, with a firm reliance on the protection of Divine Providence, permanently shed themselves from the tyrannical rule of kings and determined that they were, and of right ought to be, free.

Washington waited until the last of the British forces had retreated before he was willing to depart for home. On December 23 he reported to Congress, and there he resigned his commission. He informed Congress that he intended to take leave of all employments of public life, dispelling any remaining suspicion that he might still be persuaded to rule as king.

Returning absolute power back to the people was indeed a rare moment in history. Many were astonished at this singular act. In London, King George III questioned an American about what Washington would do now that he had won the war:

"Oh," he responded, *"They say he will return to Mount Vernon to farm and live out his life as a private citizen."* King George stated in amazement, *"If he does that, he will be the greatest man in the world."*

This singular act by Washington told mankind that America would not be ruled by earthly kings, but that our King would be the God of Heaven.

"Washington Resigns His Commission"

"*The Most Able Among Them*"

"The Most *Able* Among Them"
James Madison

The American people, wise from experience, were prepared for self-government; however, their first constitution, The Articles of Confederation, was a failure. Congress had not yet discovered the balance between tyranny and anarchy.

The entire American experiment was falling to pieces. The unity that existed during the war had all but disappeared. The states treated one another as foreign countries.

Such hostility had developed that New England was threatening to secede from the Union! And what's worse, the southern states were saying good riddance.

The whole civilized world was watching to see if this young nation would survive. From all appearances, each state seemed prepared to go their separate ways.

When the Founding Fathers assembled in Philadelphia in May of 1787, it was a frightening experience due to the political weaknesses that vexed the nation. Fortunately the states sent 55 of their most outstanding statesmen.

Aside from George Washington, James Madison was the most important delegate to the convention. Long study had given him an almost prophetic quality. In the months prior to the convention, Madison had requested books from Thomas Jefferson. In response, the books arrived, not in ones or twos, but by the hundreds. The other delegates believed that "Madison was the most able among them." His long study and deep understanding of government allowed him to prepare fifteen resolutions that were discussed, debated, and essentially became the Constitution.

"A Constitution for the Ages"

"A *Constitution* FOR THE AGES"

JAMES MADISON

On the opening day of the convention, Madison took a seat at the front of the room to more clearly hear and observe the proceedings. Day after day, for four months, one would see him there, at the front of the room, bowed over his notes, writing steadily. Never absent and exceedingly dedicated, Madison's notes on the debates of the Constitutional Convention were carried out with exactness and meticulous care—giving history a priceless record of the proceedings.

❖

But such dedication oft-times demands a price—during the course of his tireless work, Madison became quite ill; at one point during the convention he withered to less than 100 pounds, and still he labored on, with a determination to create a constitution for the ages.

Tuesday, May 29, after delegations from nine states had arrived, Governor Randolph of Virginia arose and introduced the *"Fifteen Resolves"* prepared by Mr. Madison.

This marked the beginning of a remarkable event that had never before occurred in history. A people sent their best and brightest to unite under one purpose and under one faith, to work out their own form of self-government with wisdom and purpose, not by force or conquest.

"James Wilson of Pennsylvania"

Building CONSENSUS AT THE CONSTITUTIONAL CONVENTION

$\longleftrightarrow$

*T*extbooks mistakenly describe the Constitution as a *"conglomerate of compromises."* Compromise can be an ugly word—a grinding down of the best to suit the worst. Yet in the Constitutional Convention the spirit of consensus, after much debate, reigned in grace and glory; it sat on Washington's shoulder like a dove as he presided over the proceedings.

An example of reaching consensus came at one point during the convention when Governor Randolph stood up and said, *"There should be three presidents; one for the northern states, one for the central states, and one for the southern states because there is safety in numbers."*

"Safety in numbers!" exclaimed James Wilson of Pennsylvania. *"Safety in numbers! Have you forgotten the thirty tyrants of Greece?"*

The thirty tyrants of Greece came to power after the war with Sparta. When thirty people are in charge and something goes wrong, who gets the blame?—the other twenty-nine. James Wilson explained this problem and Governor Randolph conceded, *"Perhaps you are right, we should have only one executive."*

Although it took over sixty votes just to determine how to elect the President, they talked it out, overcame pride, put away prejudices, thought it through and came to consensus. Men rose to speak, men who carried with them the biases of birthright, local issues, and loyalty to their state—North against South, merchant against farmer. But the delegates all came with one central goal—to form a limited government based on natural, unalienable rights, where all power originates from the people.

Under the rule of a king, America experienced the oppressive arm of tyranny. The loose, weak government under the Articles of Confederation protected their rights no better as America approached anarchy. Freedom was proving difficult, but history had shown that taking away Liberty had never been the solution to those difficulties. Only a perfect balance between tyranny and anarchy would provide the solution they sought. The balance was eventually found as they unified in the spirit of consensus.

THE "*Crisis* PERIOD" AT THE CONSTITUTIONAL CONVENTION

Unity was not always an easy task during the Constitutional Convention. After June 19, 1787, the delegates tried to probe some of the more prickly questions which had previously been postponed. For five weeks the convention was on the brink of failure, a time known as the *"Crisis Period."*

The most stubborn debate was regarding representation in the legislative branch. As the lawmaking and taxing branch of government, the delegates agreed to divide it into two houses, a Senate and a House of Representatives.

James Madison's Virginia Resolutions called for the number of representatives in each house to be based on the population of each state—the larger the state, the more representatives, and the more senators. This was fine for the large states but the smaller states' voices would be unheard in the new Congress.

"Surely," James Madison argued, *"you can see, the people, not the states, must be represented."*

John Dickenson and Gunning Bedford of Delaware fired back, *"No, Mr. Madison, we cannot see. You wish to strip Delaware of her equal voice. Virginia's population would give her sixteen times more representation. Each state must have an equal vote in congress."*

"If the votes be equal," Madison returned, *"Delaware will have sixteen times more representation than Virginia. The people must be represented equally, not the states."*

Delaware responded in a proud posture, *"Your plan calls for a federation of states, equal and sovereign. The states must have an equal vote or they will be swallowed up by an overpowering federal government, and with that, Mr. Madison, your plan will fail. The federal government must be kept within narrow limits, to preserve the state governments, not to govern individuals."*

Fire and water themselves are more compatible than the fervent debate which divided the large and small states. The heated debate caused a deadlock for weeks. It was during this dark crisis period that Washington wrote:

"I almost despair of seeing a favorable issue to the proceedings of the Convention, and do therefore repent having had any agency in the business."

Observers said he looked as grim as when he was at Valley Forge.

Some progress was made as they unanimously agreed to have the Senate elected by the state legislatures to serve as a check against the people's House of Representatives. All agreed that the Senate should represent the states in the new government. However, the debate on proportional representation was relentless; they voted again and again and could not break the deadlock.

"If we do not concede on both sides," said North Carolina, *"our business must soon be at an end."*

"It seems we have got to a point," said Roger Sherman, *"that we cannot move one way or another."*

Washington realized that there must be a compromise. It was time for the large states to yield, but Madison refused. He received a sharp rebuke from Washington, *"I will not see this convention crumble around me because the brightest and stubbornest of us will not yield the Senate to the states."*

Roger Sherman advanced an idea that brought the small states closer to compromise than any other speech on the floor. He proposed that the House of Representatives be elected by the people, the number of representatives to be based on the population of the states—to satisfy the large states. On the other hand, each state would be equally represented by two Senators—to satisfy the small states. This *"Great Compromise"* finally passed by a narrow margin and allowed the convention to depart from the heated exchange that threatened the whole cause.

The significance of the Great Compromise was not readily apparent, but time would soon reveal a miracle that was forged from that fiery furnace of debate, a new kind of nation, one such as Madison and the others had never considered—a national government that is strong and sovereign, but a federation of states that are also strong and sovereign; separate states but a united people.

No law or resolution can be passed without the concurrence, first, of a majority of the people, and then, of a majority of the States. The people are represented in the House of Representatives to protect the interests of the majority, while the states are represented in the Senate to protect the interests of the states. This system reserves to the states sufficient power against the federal government to protect the individual rights of their citizens from the tyranny of a federal government.

Madison expressed, *"I do not know whether such a creature can survive in the rough and tumble of the world, but I am willing to make the hazard. I am for the United States of America."*

The unique federal structure formulated in convention endured to protect the rights of the people and the states until 1913, when the Seventeenth Amendment outlawed the election of Senators by the state legislatures and placed it with the masses. Both the House of Representatives and the Senate now represent the same interests and the state legislatures no longer have the power to check the federal government. The Seventeenth Amendment has singularly eroded the Founders' original formula more than any other action. In the not-too-distant future, America may need to reevaluate a return to the Founders' original system that was so thoroughly vetted in the refiner's fire of debate.

A *Plea* FOR PRAYER
BENJAMIN FRANKLIN

*I*t was during the crisis period that 81 year-old Benjamin Franklin made his famous plea for prayer:

"Gentlemen, Gentlemen, the little progress we have made in the last weeks is a melancholy proof of the imperfections of the human understanding; groping as it were in the dark, how has it happened that we have not sought the Father of lights to illuminate our understanding? In the beginning of the war with Britain we had daily prayer in this [very] room, and asked for divine protection. Our prayers were heard; and they were graciously answered. And have we now forgotten that powerful Friend? Or do we imagine that we no longer need His assistance?

"I have lived, sir, a long time; and the longer I live the more covincing proofs I see of this truth—that God governs in the affairs of men. And if a sparrow cannot fall to the ground without His notice, is it probable that an empire can rise without His aid? We have been assured, in the sacred writings, that 'except the Lord build the house they labor in vain that build it.'

"I, therefore, beg leave to move, that hereafter prayers, imploring the assistance of Heaven and its blessing on our deliberations, be held in this assembly every morning before we proceed to business."

Franklin's plea had a sobering effect on the delegates, and they set about their task with greater determination.

"George Mason of Virginia"

Bill OF RIGHTS
GEORGE MASON

On Monday, September 17, 1787, forty-one delegates solemnly met in the east room of Independence Hall for the signing. As the convention was coming to a close, George Mason rose to his feet and said,

"I would rather cut off my right hand than to put it to that document."

"But Colonel Mason," James Madison plead,
"Why at this late hour would you not sign it?"

"Because it does not have a Bill of Rights," Mason replied.

*"But Colonel Mason, we have not given the Federal Government
enough power to trample our rights."*

His answer was classic, *"But they will, they always do."*

This too, was a concern among the states and many proposed changes were submitted at the first session of Congress. Twelve of the amendments were approved by Congress and submitted to the states. Ten were ratified and became the famous American Bill of Rights.

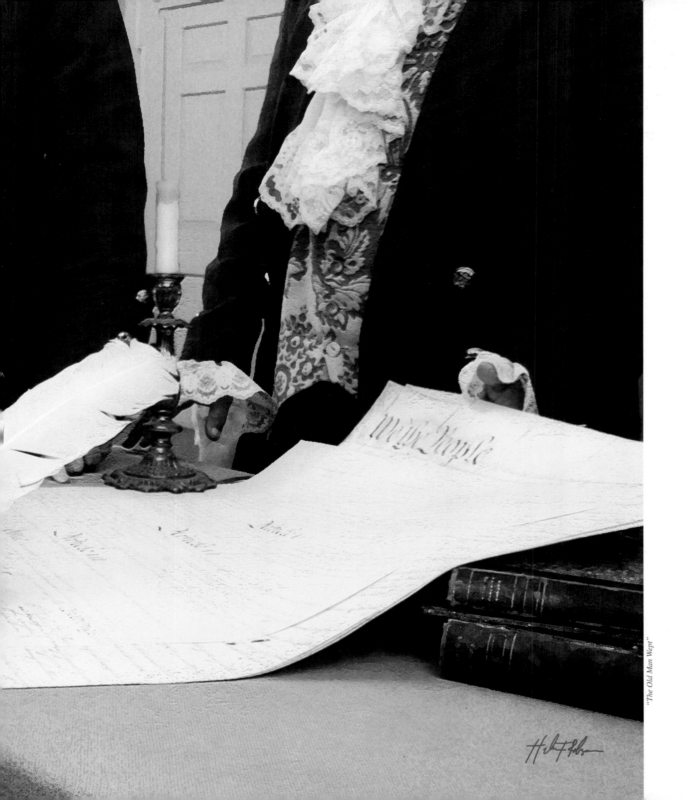

"The Old Man Wept"

"THE _Old_ MAN WEPT"
BENJAMIN FRANKLIN

As the delegates were signing, James Madison carefully watched each of them.

One by one they reverently arose, approached Washington's desk, dipped their quill and placed their names on that inspired work.

Benjamin Franklin had been trying to unite the colonies for decades; now at the close of his life he not only watched it take place but applied his wisdom to the proceedings. When Franklin signed it was recorded:

"The old man wept."

53

"A *Rising* Sun"
BENJAMIN FRANKLIN

"A Rising Sun"

A s the last signers placed their hand to the document, Franklin referred to a carving of a sun on the back of George Washington's chair and said:

"I have . . . often, in the course of the session . . . looked at that [sun] behind the president without being able to tell whether it was rising or setting. But now at length I have the happiness to know that it is a rising and not a setting sun."

55

THE *Miracle* AT PHILADELPHIA

"*The Miracle at Philadelphia*"

*T*he collection of men who attended the Constitutional Convention was truly a miracle. They were raised up for this very purpose. They did not consider their post as a position of gain and glory, but rather they humbly considered it a position of honor. Major William Pierce, a delegate from Georgia, expressed that sentiment when he said:

"The ... flattering opinion which some of my friends had of me ... gave me a seat in the wisest council in the world."

The Constitutional Convention was a miracle. It united a group of men that were among the most honorable and intelligent the world has ever known. They came together and framed a government based on the majesty of God's law.

The Declaration of Independence and the Constitution of the United States of America formed our nation into a heritage of belief, faith and trust in the Creator. The colonists called upon Him, *and He answered*. The common man invoked His divine help, *and He answered*. The founders sought wisdom, *and He answered*. These two documents can solve every problem facing our country today.

These are the miracles of our nation. This is our heritage. With His divine aid and our renewed faith the miracles will continue!

Read more about the inspiring lives of those who helped shape our nation in the *American Classic Series* by the

National Center for Constitutional Studies

"Every child in America should be acquainted with his own country. He should read books that furnish him with ideas that will be useful to him in life and practice. As soon as he opens his lips, he should rehearse the history of his own country."   -Noah Webster, 1788

The Real George Washington
The True Story of America's Most Indispensable Man

Rather than focus on the interpretations of historians, *The Real George Washington* tells much of the true story of George Washington's life in his own words. He was the dominant personality in three of the most critical events in the founding of America: the Revolutionary War, the Constitutional Convention, and the first national administration. The second part of this book brings together the most important and insightful passages from Washington's writings, conveniently arranged by subject.

The Real Benjamin Franklin
The True Story of America's Greatest Diplomat

Benjamin Franklin has been portrayed as a hard-headed businessman, a prankster, a renowned scientist, a British spy, a loyal patriot, a lecherous womanizer, and a man of deep religious convictions. *The Real Benjamin Franklin* cuts through the confusion and lets us meet the man as he really was—rather than as he has been characterized by historians. The book tells much of his exciting story in his own words. The second part of this book brings together the most important and insightful passages from Franklin's writings, conveniently arranged by subject.

The Real Thomas Jefferson
The True Story of America's Philosopher of Freedom

The Real Thomas Jefferson is the true story of America's Philosopher of Freedom. This book lets you meet the man as he really was—rather than as interpreted by historians—as much of this exciting story is told in his own words. The second part of this book brings together the most important and insightful passages from Jefferson's writings, conveniently arranged by subject.

To order these and other publications contact
National Center for Constitutional Studies
37777 West Juniper Road, Malta, Idaho 83342
208-645-2625   www.nccs.net

NATIONAL CENTER FOR CONSTITUTIONAL STUDIES
www.nccs.net